DOMESTIC VIOLENCE IN RURAL INDIA

A STUDY OF A VILLAGE IN HARYANA

TEKMAL SOLMANRAJ

Made with ♥ on the Notion Press Platform
www.notionpress.com

TO

GOD

PARENTS, NEAR AND DEAR ONES

Contents

Foreword

Its my immense pleasure to write foreward for this wonderful book which shows real anguish, sorrow and sadness of the victims of the domestic violence in India. A study of a village in Haryana. it brings ligt in the perspective of socio- Psycological and cultural aspect to know the plight of the victims. In this book author systemetically structured the real and pathetic condition of the victims, so i would like to suggest every one to read and understand the condition of victims and contribute to the victims from your end

Prof. Anil Kumar Singh Jha
Department of Sociological Studies
Central University of South Bihar, Gaya, India

Preface

We are so much excited to introduce a wonderful book "Domestic Violence in India" A Study of A Village in Haryana. which shows the real grief and heart breaks of the victims of the domestic violence in India. Here we can see different age groups and different relations present in the context, This book will be throwing light on the issues from the socio-psychological and cultural perspective. The majority of the victims are the family members of the alcohol consumers.Here in this book we will be discussing on other forms of the violence such as physical, mental and sexual violence, we would like to encourage you to go through this book and understand the problelms of victims in india and we have given some suggestions to eradicate domestic violence, hence we are strongly encouraging you to help and suport the victims at your end

Mr. Tekmal Solmanraj
Ms. Arshi Khanam
Ms. Preeti Sharma

Acknowledgements

we would like to Express our special thanks and gratitude to our respondants (Victims of domestic violence) This book not have been possible without their support.

contents

1

Introduction

The term domestic violence consists of two terms. One is 'Domestic' which refers to "inside the realm or domestic region," and another one is 'Violence' which refers "using physical force to wound and cause damage". As a result, "domestic violence" is defined as a "series of coercive and assaultive behaviours against an intimate partner, including physical, sexual, verbal and psychological attacks , as well as economic pressure."Thus, domestic violence is rarely a one-time event, and it is the use of threats, intimidation, manipulation, and physical violence by someone wanting power and control over their personal relationships on a large scale. Domestic violence against women is a phenomenon that cuts across culture, religion, class, and, ethnicity.

Domestic abuse is not commonly acknowledged and has remain unseen despite its ubiquitous nature. Due to the social creation of the barrier between public and private matters, domestic abuse against women remains hidden. The house has always been regarded as the realm of the male-head of the household, who has absolute control and authority over it. Domestic violence is the most serious violation of a woman's fundamental rights that she faces in her own home at the hands of family members. Data and in-depth work done by several people in the women"s movement have systematically exposed to many problems associated with domestic violence. Indeed, the home has been identified as a site of violence against women and girls in recent studies by the Family Health Survey and the National Crimes Record Bureau. A young married woman is burnt alive, beaten to death, or forced to commit suicide almost every six hours somewhere in India.

Domestic violence has serious consequences for the health and well-being of individual women, but it also serves to maintain their subjugation as a class. At least 20% of married women between the ages of 15 and 49 have experienced domestic violence at some point in their lives. Domestic violence has serious consequences for the health and well-being of individual women, but it also serves to maintain their subjugation as a class. In general, it denies women their individual rights.. Furthermore, the existence of domestic abuse is not even acknowledged by the law. Domestic violence is still a problem that can be resolved within the four walls of a home, and some violence is considered typical ""wear and tear"" in marriage. Changes in society, however, are inevitable, and they may not always be for the best. Atrocities against women are on the rise, to the point where daily newspaper columns are brimming with accounts of child and woman abuse, as well as women"s murders or suicides as a result of failing to meet the greedy demands of their husbands or relatives.This is a common misunderstanding.

A crucial component is that a woman may be subjected to violence only once during one of her life-cycle stages, or she may be exposed to several episodes of violence at different times throughout her life. Domestic violence, on the other hand, has been proven beyond a shadow of a doubt to be one of the world's most prevalent types of violence against women. Women are subjected to violence from the moment they are conceived until the end of their lives.Thus, the situation of continued and escalating violence against women is one the most important hurdles to their growth. This is a significant infringement on the human rights of women. Female foeticide and infanticide ,infanticide, sexual abuse ,incest abuse, incest, molestation ,sexual molestation, sexual harassment at work and on the streets, marital rape, and domestic violence in the form of wife assault and woman battering are only a few examples of gender violence. Due to unmet dowry demands, millions of women are harassed, and many are killed or pushed to death. As a result, violence against women plays a major, yet under appreciated role in the phenomenon of women"s marginalisation in the development process.

A female, minor or adult, is always under guardianship, while single, she is under the aegis of her father, if he is dead, of other male relatives. After her marriage, she comes under the protection of her husband; until his death. Given the strength of patriarchy in rural areas, this men control over women is never slackened throughout her life. Its more change of authority from that of her father and brother to her husband and son. This ideology of guardianship, control, and dependence, however small, is considered to be very threatening. A man's honor is predicated largely on his ability to impose this control over his women folk. This means that she has no control over her own self. All decisions regarding her body must be made by the male members of her family-the upholder of her honor. Violence is associated with masculinity and hence is normal rather than an aberration. In any case, violence against women in the home sphere-as daughter, sister, wife and mother has widespread acceptance and social legitimacy under patriarchy (Prem Chowdhry, 2007:16-17) Choudhary continue to argues that "both men and women embody notion of honor, but differently, the woman or the repository and the man is the regulated of this honor therefore, the greatest danger to the ideology of honor comes from the women. One oft-repeated phrase is: *Ladki ke sath uske kutumb ki izzat judi huee hai. Honor* so posited in a woman is, importantly, located in her body. A woman dishonors her family by what is considered her shameful physical behavior" (Ibid 2007: 16). "The women saw their batterer's and their father's attitudes toward women as similar, their mother's and non batterer are as more liberal than the other but less show than their own".

It is assumed that the batterer's control forced the battered women behave in a more traditional way than they state would prefer" (Walker, 2017:12). In patriarchal organization of society facilitates and may even reward wife abuse, some men live up to their violent potential while other do not. Patriarchal organization is traditional where sex role in stereotyped order. A traditional man have more expectation from his wife thus if she does not have his dinner on the table when he returns home from work , even if she also has worked outside the home, he believes she does not care for him . This is also the reason of violence. women thinks that if they are not doing work according to her partner they will be kill by them. They have fear in their mind that's why they do whatever the man demands. Battering incidents starts and stops at home. Often starting in the living room, kitchen, or bedroom, and ending in the same room in which they started (Walker, 2017:53)

Violence is an extremely sensitive issue. Violence is the use of physical force or power against a person. Violence is a problem in today's world. Violence happens all over world. It is the aggressive behavior of individual. The World Health Organization (WHO) defines violence as the use of physical force or power, threatened against oneself. Violence presents an ugly image of themselves and their partner who act violently. Violence is shocking, horrible and life threatening. Violence is an expression of aggression. Violence can impact various forms of human life. Violence hurt not only physically but emotionally and psychologically. Anybody whether men, women or children can be the victim of domestic violence (Krantz Gunilla, 2005:818-820). According to Lenore Walker, " Violence does not come from the interaction of the partners in the relationship, nor from provocation caused by possibly irritating personality traits of the battered women, rather ,the violence comes from the batterers learned behavioral response" (Walker, 2017: 19).

1. Violence and Abuse

Abuse can take many forms and violence is one of them. Violence is the use of physical force or power against a person. Violence is the form of the abusive behavior. For example abusive behavior happen in many ways like in verbal abuse, a person put downs another person Like- how can you be so stupid, you look so ugly etc,.It uses threats and manipulative etc.

"Physical abuse" refers to any act or conduct that causes bodily pain, harm, or danger to life, limb, or health, or impairs the aggrieved person's health or development, and includes assault, criminal intimidation, and criminal force.

"Sexual abuse" refers to any sexual behaviour that abuses, humiliates, degrades, or otherwise violates the dignity of a woman.

"Verbal and emotional abuse" includes (a) insults, ridicule, humiliation, and name calling, as well as (b) repeated threats to cause physical pain to anyone the aggrieved person is interested in.

Violence is the sub-category of abuse. Violence is a form of physical abuse. It generally refer to the act of harming another person (Eisikovits, 2000:5) There are different types of violence and this book focuses on domestic violence against women.

Forms of Violence

1. **Mental Violence**

Mental abuse is a form of violence that affects the mind, often leaving the abused feeling worthless and lacking empowerment.. Threat, Fear, threat to harm children, Isolation from family and friends, Loss of social contact, Persistent criticism, denial of privacy, verbal abuse, deprivation of sleep, money, clothes, going out, use of telephone, terror and intimidation.

2. Physical Violence

Physical violence is called as aggressive acts such as throwing things, kicking, slapping, hitting, Pushing, shoving, grabbing, Choking, strangling, suffocating, using a weapon, bruising, breaking bones, cuts, scratches, Bitting, burnt, scalded, Knocking unconscious, Miscarriage due to violence,throwing Chemical on face, and death. In the physical violence women are injured seriously and in some cases are dead. According a studied from various part of the world shows that between 10% and 60% of the women had been hit and physically assaulted by their male partner (Garcia Moreno: 2005)

3. Sexual Violence

In this, women are exploited by their male partner. This type of violence happens everywhere. Male partner forced his wife have to have sex. This leads to rape, sexual assault, degrading and humiliating all the acts come in this type of violence.

4. Verbal violence

Verbal abuse occurs when "one person uses any words or body language to inappropriately criticize another person," observed Patricelli. (Abrahams, 2007:18) Verbal abuse is characterized as a mental abuse because the abuser will taunt the abused, making her feel unloved and unworthy of respect. Verbal abusing also painful and damaging and it's also affecting the women life. In verbal abuse you feel afraid and powerless. Verbal abuse includes name calling, putting you down, rejecting your opinions, insulting, blaming and mocking.

5. Emotional violence

Emotional abuse is a type of abuse in which ones play with someone's emotions. There is many ways in which your partner control and manipulate your emotions. In emotional violence include the yelling or swearing, name calling, insult, ignoring. This type of violence is difficult to define like; husband forces to his wife to have sex

6. Other Forms of Violence

Damage to personal property, theft of property, threats and violence to pets, animals, denied access to work.Domestic violence happens in personal relationship domestic violence is abusive behavior in which a partner controls another partner. It may happen between current partner, girlfriend and boyfriend, men and women of any religion and any race affected by domestic violence. But most of its victims are women. Violence is the big problem facing by our society today. Alcohol playing a important role in these violence. Hence we can say that violent behaviour is like as drinking behaviour, violence happens both physical and mental. Violence against women is being recognized as an important public health concern. Emotional sexual and physical violence by an intimate male partner is one of the most common forms it takes In India, where family structure is patriarchal, patrilocal and patrilineal, women are particularly vulnerable to violence.

In contemporary households, male-dominated hierarchies influence the decision-making power in all domestic spheres: economic, social and sexual. Alcohol consumption is related to intimate partner and sexual violence through multiple channels. By increasing aggression and heightening emotional responses, alcohol use may increase inter-gender violence. Domestic violence includes violence against any number of house-hold; violence faced by married women within their conjugal home is the focus of this paper. Husbands do violence against women. Men think that they are superior to women.

they have right to control women's behavior. Violence is a form of extended belief that men have the right to control women's behavior. Violence also includes harm to women health, whether mental or physical. It may be through physical, sexual, verbal, emotional and economic abuse.

In more traditional society's wife beating is man's right in many developing countries women agrees with that type of idea that men have the right to discipline their wives with force. Indian culture also permit male for controlling women's behavior. For example, one statement is found in North India, "If it is a great mistake, then the husband is justified in beating his wife. Why not? A cow will not be obedient without beating."Studies from industrialized and developing countries produced a list of events which are responsible for violence women are not obeying her man. Women does not offers food on time, if she questions about his money and girlfriends, if she is going somewhere without the man's permission, refusing the man to sex. (Buchbindereli, 2000:16-17) There are many factors which are responsible for domestic violence like younger age, lower educational level, a history of physical violence in the family, childhood sexual abuse, depression, poor socio-economic conditions and problems, related to alcohol consumption among one or both family of the couple.

Culture plays a key role in abusive relationship, our socialization tells what a girl can do and what a boy can do. Society fixed our roles. It also said that boys are more aggressive than girls. In general women are not equal to men. Men are active and women are passive.

3. Patriarchy: The Common Factor

Patriarchy plays an important role in domestic violence. Due to patriarchy violence is practiced in the society. Patriarchy is a Greek word. its mean the role of the father. Where the male dominated society. According to Radical feminist, "It is analysis of gender inequality in which men as a group dominate women as a group and are the main beneficiaries of the subordination of women. This system of domination is called patriarchy" (Walby Sylvia, 1986). According to Sylvia, patriarchy provides a system of control and law and order. She also interlinked patriarchy and capitalist. Both capitalist and patriarchy, argues that both system are present and important in the structuring of contemporary gender relations. Capitalist and patriarchy are two system that are so closed, patriarchy provides a system of control and law and order, while capitalism provides a system of economy, the pursuit of profit (Ibid: 5). According to Dolphy, "Housewives constitute one class and husbands, another. They have a relation of economic difference and of social inequality. She argues that housewives are the producing class, engaged in domestic labour, while husbands are the non-producing class, expropriating the labour of their wives" (Walby cited in Dolphy, 1986). Patriarchy as a system of social structure and practice in which men dominate, oppress and exploit women. Women work as a day to day worker for no wage, such as food and cleans clothes, and for producing the next generation of worker. (Ibid: 21). Gerda Lerner in her book talks about the patriarchy. According to her, the notion of 'exchange of women' defines how people saw women as a thing and not a human being. Men always see the profit in this system in terms of marriages, and sexual services. For example in Mesopotamian societies, the people who are poor sold their daughter into marriages and prostitution for economic profit. She also said that male dominance over women is not natural or biological but it begun in ancient time. The system of patriarchy can function only with the cooperation of women. For example, educational deprivation, gender base biasness, discrimination and political power (Lerner 211-213).

According to Aristotle, the male principle is active and the female is passive, also for him, female was a mutilated male, someone who does not have a soul. The male is superior and the female is inferior, men are born to rule and women are born to be ruled. Under patriarchy different kind of violence is practiced. Feminist also believe that violence against women is not just pervasive. It is a system in patriarchy (Kamla Bhasin, 2000:10). Girls are expected that they should behave in a proper manner. In India there is a patriarchal system. The society is male dominated; violence is also occurred by male. India is not homogeneous. There exist a variety of cultural norms which affects the caste, gender roles towards domestic violence. Some feminist saw that domestic violence also occurred in dowry system like beating and harassing a young wife in demanding more dowry's from her family side.

The violence against women also increases because of alcohol. Women go through violence because her husband is habitual of consumption of alcohol. This excessive drinking leads to partner violence. There is a big relation between alcohol and violence. National Criminal Victimization Survey (1991) perceived more than one fourth of violent criminal to be under the influences of alcohol (Robert and Kathleen, 1998:293). Many studies relate to violence and alcohol consumption. A study in Brazil found that alcohol consumption increases the violent behavior and the anger of a person also increases. A population based study in Brazil found that aggressor was under the influence of alcohol at the time of the event in over half of the identified cases of domestic violence. Violence becomes more dangerous with increased alcohol consumption. Alcohol is the risk for the violent behavior because it has direct effects on the person, reducing self-control, reducing judgments, reducing the ability to recognize signs of danger. Alcohol affects the family members, children and other relatives influenced by alcoholism. Many cases of domestic violence happens due to insecurity if the spouses are either suspected or are unfaithful.

"Studies from Australia, Canada, Israel, South Africa and the United States Of America shows that 40-70% of female murder victims were killed by their husbands and boyfriends" (Buchbinder, 2000)

"According to United Nation Population Fund Report`, "around two –third of married women in India between the age of 15 and 49 are victims of beating, rape or forced sex. In India, more than 55 percent of the women suffer from Domestic Violence, especially in the state of Bihar, U.P., M.P., and other northern states"(Pahuja, 2011).

Alcoholism is the problem of an individual. Alcoholism is seen as stressful experience in the family. Life is very challenging for alcoholic spouses. They are forced to cope up with the stress and also helping a person who is physically affected. When, in a family a person who is addicted to alcohol, the whole family is affected. Alcohol affects the mental health of the family. Alcohol also affects the physical health. Physical health of an alcoholic person is not well. In ancient time scriptures described wife enjoyed a status equal to her husband. Woman was the half of man, the best of his friends.

According to Indian system, marriage is a holy sacrament. Universally marriage is one of the most intimate and socially recognized interpersonal domains. In the marriage system, two people share their present, past and future. The couple has legal, emotional, financial and many other responsibilities towards each-other. Women were largely responsible for providing an ensuring and for a decent home Their husband were happy and satisfied. This could be meant that women were expected to serve their husband sexually and domestically (J. Jeffrey's: 1990).

Alcohol affects the alcoholic person. Many studies show that both heavy drinking and drinking problems related to age and gender. Young men are most at risk although young adults are at greater risk than others.

According to NAFVS (National Alcohol and Family Violence Survey 1992) the empirical evidence shows that the linkage between drinking and wife bearing are not a problem of poor ethnic minorities. Domestic violence due to alcohol consumptions are recognized as major public health problems. Domestic violence and alcohol both are biological, psychological and sociological factors. Alcohol consumption is the third leading risk factor for illness and disabilities worldwide (WHO). Alcohol can affect the individual health due to accidents, dependence, live cancer and injury. Alcohol consumption also affects the health of other people and family. Due to drinking and driving situations work absenteeism.

Domestic violence is a major health problem. Violence has serious effect on health, psychological and social development of individuals. Domestic violence is physical psychological, sexual violence. In the family, violence can happen within interpersonal relationships including children, adolescents, men, women and elderly. Domestic violence include young age, a history of physical violence in the family, lower educational level, depression, poor socio-economic condition, childhood and sexual abuse.

"There is a great link between alcohol use and violence against intimate partner. Evidence shows that alcohol increases the violence. Alcohol uses directly affect physical function, reducing self- control. The WHO multi-country study on women's health and domestic violence against women law data are here that between 15% (Japan) and 71% (Ethiopia) of women reported physical and sexual violence by an intimate partner over their lifetime and between 3.8%(Japan) and 53% (Ethiopia) as experiencing that such violence within the past year. In a survey of 24000 men and women in Canada, 7% of women and 6% of men operated having been victims of intimate partner violence in the last 5 years. Individual beliefs that alcohol causes aggression and encourages violent behavior after drinking. Children are the witnesses of violence or threats of violence between parents."(WHO, Alcohol & violence: 4). Drugs and alcohol is increasing the human tendency towards aggression. The direct effects of alcohol and drugs are on domestic violence.

"For the victim health effects including physical, injury, emotional problems are leading to suicide, depression. Around us 11% of all Homicides between 1976 and 2002 committed by an intimate partner victim relationship with family is also affected. Model of alcohol and domestic violence and women abuse as rooted in men's drive for power or others.(Gondola,1995) the increased unpredictability of a man's behavior while drunk or stoned observed over time and increases the chances that a woman will behave according to a men will because of fear for her safety. Some violence by man against women is motivated not by the desire to express anger, frustration over some other immediate emotion during a family conflict but by the desire to control however the use of violence may indicate not the experience of domination but it is the same time a major of its imperfection (Connell 1995:84). Many men who assault their partners because they have fear that their control is breaking down (Intimate partner violence and alcohol, WHO, 2005)

A woman is beaten by a man. They live in violence, and yet they remain together. They view themselves as a couple. Domestic violence destroys the women's emotional and social world. Domestic violence occurs behind closed doors and thrives in environment isolation. In domestic violence a woman who is paying a heavy personal, social, economic and emotional cost. For any woman who is in a violent relationship seeking to leave it or trying to find the strength to rebuild her life. There is not only practical support but also emotional support.

2

Literature Review

A review of the literature is an essential component of every research project because it serves as the foundation for the research. It also aids in the discovery of gaps in previous research and present research. Women's issues have got a lot of attention from social scientists during the last few decades. A vast number of studies have been undertaken in India and overseas on the many facets of domestic violence. Domestic violence against women is a broad term, as the types, causes, and effects vary from society and from time.

Domestic violence, also known as intimate partner violence (IPV), is one of the most horrific crimes that may be committed in any community. These instances are particularly delicate because the perpetrators are often family members or who are close to the victim, such as husbands and in-laws. They are sometimes known as "silent abusers" since they occur behind closed doors with few witnesses. Women's violence has become a widespread problem in India, with devastating physical, sexual, emotional, psychological, and economic effects for women.The reason for this discussion is that understanding the causes of such offences is important because the various causes that start a fight at home behind closed doors should be carefully examined, and studying the various factors that cause such criminal acts can aid in preventing a family from suffering the harmful effects of domestic violence. Domestic abuse was made illegal in India in the early 1980s as a result of a persistent campaign by feminist organisations and women's activists across the country. After the widely panned Tukaram v. State of Maharashtra decision, the movement gained significant momentum.

Davis (1998) The term "battered" is used by the author of the book "Battered Women: Implications for Social Changes" (1988) to describe the situation of women who have been victims of domestic abuse. In his work, the author emphasises his concern about the subject, claiming that "cases of domestic violence and beatings of women occur in personal relationships, particularly within the household". He goes on to say that marital rape, death threats, torture, and harassment, as well as slapping, beating, striking, and poking, are all forms of battering against women.

Sharma (2006)A book about domestic abuse in India is titled "Behind Closed Doors: Domestic Violence in India" (2006). The most humiliating experience for a woman, in the words of Kaveri Sharma, "is to be assaulted, used, and raped by someone as intimate as a spouse." Women who are the victims of these crimes frequently aren't aware that domestic abuse is a recognised crime and that it happens frequently in India. The author draws attention to the fact that women's voices are frequently suppressed by their society, family, morals, and customs. They are taken for granted, and since they never object or voice dissent, their muted cries of terror and trauma are kept behind the four walls of the house, escaping the ears of security or law enforcement personnel.

The author explores numerous approaches to dealing with domestic violence or abusive relationships in another book, "Overcoming a Life of Domestic Violence and Abusive Relationships" (2015). Many variables are discussed throughout the book in order to assist a victim of such abuse in overcoming and rehabilitating themselves after such abuse. The author has covered a number of topics in depth, including how to forget the past and move forward; the advantages of starting a new and fresh life; the causes of domestic violence; where a victim can seek help in the event of such an experience; and the difficult times when a woman isolates herself as a result of such abuse.

Rachel Louise Synder used the phrase 'intimate terrorism' in her book"NoVisible Bruises - What We don't Know About Domestic Violence Can Kill Us" (2019). Despite the fact that the World Health Organization has labelled the crime a "global epidemic," the author claims that none of us believe it has anything to do with us because it is a private problem between couples. The book is a collection of actual accounts of women who have been victims of domestic violence. The in-depth examination of the crimes and the procedures used to deal with them provides a disturbing and alarming impression of the challenges that women face in America and around the world.

While discussing the historical background of the PWDV Act in Chapter 2 of the book – "Socio Economic Offences in India" edited by Ratan Singh and Virender Singh" (2021). Virender Singh stated that the police always used discretion in avoiding arrest when responding to domestic violence incidents. There are complaints in many police stations, policies for DV or domestic disputes actively discourage arrests, focusing instead on responses such as clerical or administrative removal. Domestic violence convictions face less severe sentences, which explains why more domestic violence cases are dismissed at the prosecution stage than other types of violent crimes. Whether or not any other relief is sought in the victim's proceedings, the current DV Act is a civil statute that offers emergency and ex- parte injunctions and non-molestation orders. The legislation aims to safeguard women and children from domestic abuse perpetrated by family members.

According to INCLEN Trust International (2000), it is a problem that affects people of all ages, social classes, and educational levels. According to the report, at least 40% of married women have experienced physical violence at some point in their lives. According to Murthy, domestic violence is influenced by the husband's education, the number of family members, the type of marriage, and menstrual issues, among other factors. Alcoholism and drug misuse are additional factors that contribute to domestic violence. Men feel that using physical force against the weaker gender proves their masculinity.

The state of Uttar Pradesh is backward in terms of gender equality, according to an article titled "Masculanity, Intimate Partner Violence, and Son Preference in India: Findings from Uttar Pradesh."(2014) Its societal backwardness is due to the high rate of early marriage and violence against women. According to the findings, Uttar Pradesh has the highest proportion of males having high control over their wives and the lowest proportion of men who favour gender equality out of all the sample states.

The authors have explained many facets of DV incidents in their research article titled "Domestic Violence: The Dark

Truth of Our Society."(2013) The paper focuses on the psychological and social causes of domestic violence, including jealousy, social stress, mental illness, and marital problems. The current Domestic Violence Act was drafted with articles 14, 15, and 21 of the constitution in mind, in order to give victims of domestic violence civil law protection. The authors argue that more flexible civil and criminal remedies are required.

According to Dr. C.P. Prakasham's research report titled "Men's attitude towards sexual and domestic violence against women in selected states in India,"(2018) 16 percent of men and 28 percent of women in Uganda believe it is legitimate to beat a woman who refuses to have sexual relations with her husband. Sexual violence between spouses was particularly widespread in rural Uttar Pradesh, with 21% of women suffering physical abuse and 68 percent suffering sexual coercion.

The authors of the essay titled "Addressing Domestic Violence against Women: An Unfinished Agenda"(2007) have described in detail the health consequences of DV for a woman. DV has a wide range of consequences, including bodily damage as well as social, economic, psychological, spiritual, and emotional harm to the victimised woman and society as a whole. DV is a major contributor to women's health problems. It has a negative impact on women's emotional and physical health, as well as their reproductive and sexual health. Injuries, gynaecological issues, temporary or permanent disability, depression, and suicide are just a few examples.

In Kolkata, a doctoral study was undertaken on 'The implementation of the Protection of Women from Domestic Violence Act, 2005', in the context of the Kesarwani Neighbourhood, a small business community.

The study focuses on the legal construction of domestic violence acts in married relationships as well as how the legal framework exacerbates violence experienced by women in their homes and families. The research also examines how legal literacy (knowledge) and its application are primarily limited to lawyers and government officials. The general public's knowledge of the law is quite limited, and this lack of information is more prevalent in rural and interior areas of the country.

In their study, Begum et al. (2015) looked at the aggressive conduct at home among ladies in Mumbai's urban ghettos in their study "Socio-demographic characteristics related to domestic violence in urban slums, Mumbai, Maharashtra, India." A family survey was conducted among competent women. From two metropolitan ghettos, 1137 currently married women between the ages of 18 and 35 were recruited, all of whom had neglected the need for family planning and at least one child. Physical (16.8%), emotional (12.4%), and sexual brutality were all experienced by 21.2 percent of women, according to the investigation (4.8 percent). Being slapped (16.7 percent) and humiliated in front of various family members was the most common display of brutality (11.3 percent). A small percentage of women (1.9 percent) stated that their husbands forced them to perform sexual actions that they did not want to do. Ladies who married before the age of multi-year (26.8%) are more likely than those who married after the age of multi-year (18.2%) to report roughness. The prevalence of viciousness was higher among uneducated women once again. In comparison to non-SC/ST women, SC/ST women were more likely to be victims of violence. Alcoholism was also linked to a higher rate of domestic violence against women. Domestic violence was significantly connected with factors such as young marriage, the wife's job status, and the husband's alcohol consumption.

3

Research Methodology

Research Methodology.

The most important aspect of research work is its methodology. It is a part of planning or scheme which is needed at each step of the research work. When we start research work, it is necessary to follow an approved and scientific methodology for authentic data collection, data analysis and preparation of an authentic research report to be drawn out of the research work.

1. Research Objectives:

1. Is there a practice of domestic violence in Bucholi village?
2. To see whether alcoholic wife face more violence than non-alcoholic wives.
3. Is there any link between age group and violence?
4. Is there any link between educational qualifications and domestic violence?

1. Data Base:

The study is based on both primary data and secondary data. Primary data in the form of 'field work' is conducted on the women who are the victims of violence. Secondary data is based on books, journals, websites etc.

3. Research Methods:

Research methods are a way to systematically solve the research problem. It may be understood as a science of studying how research is done scientifically. In it, we study the various step which are generally adopted by a researcher in studying his research problem along with the logic behind them. It is necessary for the researcher to know not only the research methods/techniques but also the methodology." (Kothari, 2014).

Due to shortage of time, it was not specifically possible to go for qualitative study; therefore, quantitative study is also incorporated.

The study is explanatory studywhich explains the causes of social phenomena. "In simple terms, explanatory research aims at establishing a relationship between variables, i.e., how one is the cause of other or how when one variable occurs the other will also occur" (Ram Ahuja,2016)

4. Sampling methods:

When the population is relatively large and is physically not accessible, researcher survey only a sample. It is not possible to study large number of people scattered in wide geographical area. Sampling will reduce their number. Sampling saves time and money. "A sample is a portion of people drawn from a larger population. It will be representative of the population only if it has same basic characteristics of the population from which it is drawn" (Ram Ahuja, 2016). Sampling is useful to seeking data from total population covering a few units. "A sample design is a definite plan for obtaining a sample from a given population. It refers to the technique or the procedure the researcher would adopt in selecting items for the sample. Sample design may as well lay down the number of items to be included in the sample i.e., the size of the sample" (Kothari, 2014). In this research, I have used snowball sampling. The reason being that on domestic violence I have a sample/ respondents of alcoholic wife, non-alcoholic wife and old aged women which I am not quite familiar which household they fall into. So, snowball sampling, in a way was helpful to locate the respondents. In snowball sampling the researcher begins the research with the few respondents who are known and available to him. The most advantage of this sampling is it is quick and economical.

5. Universe:

A village in Mahendragarh, Haryana.

6. Sampling Sources:

In this study voter list is the sampling sources.

7. Sampling Unit:

Violence against women: a case study of a village in Haryana.

8. Unit of Analysis:

The victims (women) of domestic violence are the unit of analysis.

9. Sample Size:

The sample size refers to the number of items to be selected from the universe to constitute a sample. The size of sample should neither be excessively large, nor too small. Sample size in this study is taken from A women of a village who are the victims of domestic violence. The total population of a village is 3400. In which male population is 2000 and the female is 1400. In 1400 women, young female are 660(Above 18 and under (40), Old female are 420, 320 female are (under 18). this study took taken 250 women as sample in which 115 female are alcoholic wife, 60are non-alcoholic wife and 75 are old women .

10. Interview Schedule:

The set of structured questions in which answers are recorded by the interviewer himself is called interview schedule or simply the schedule. The questionnaire is used when the respondents are educated, the schedule can be used both for the illiterate and the educated respondents (Ram Ahuja, 2016).

Interview schedule is divided into two sections. In section I, it includes the demographic information of the respondent, in section II, it is related to the information on the perception of violence.

11. Data Processing:

Data process could be manual or electronic. It involves editing, categorizing the open-ended questions, coding, computerization and preparation of table and diagrams. After collecting the data from sampling unit, schedules were coded. Then information of these schedules was transferred in the computer. For the analysis of this study, SPSS is used. In computer software S.P.S.S (Statistical Package for the Social Sciences) is used to get the result.

12. Data analysis and interpretation:

After analysis the data, we interpret the table. Interpretation of data is also necessary. Interpretation takes the results of analysis, makes inferences and draws conclusions about the relationship. Thus, to interpret is to explain the findings.

4

Data Analysis

Domestic violence is the most serious violation of a woman's fundamental rights committed by family members in her own home. Data and in-depth work by several scholars have systematically exposed many problems associated with domestic violence. Indeed, recent studies by the Family Health Survey and the National Crimes Record Bureau have identified the home as a site of violence against women and girls.

***What is the situation of women in Haryana co-relate with do you think women of Haryana face more violence than any other state**

Table 22

		Do you think women of haryana face more violence then any other state				
		Yes	No	Can't Say	May Be	Total
	Bad	85	0	25	0	110
	Average	15	0	25	0	40
	Both bad and good	5	5	80	10	100
Total		105	5	130	10	250

Enter Caption

Data Analysis and Interpretation

The total sample is 50 which are individual. The unit of sample is individual. In which i took alcoholic wife 23, non-alcoholic wife 12 and old women are 15 alcoholic and non-alcoholic both.

The total questionnaire is 50. The information collected was cross tabulated and SPSS software was used for the data analysis. In data analysis it relates various factors with domestic violence. In this study there are total 77 questions, which were used for collecting the information from the respondents.

Out of 77 questions only 22 questions were cross tabulated. In table 1 and 2 show the number of respondent and their caste. Table 3 caste cross tabulation with educational qualification, age at marriage cross tabulation with domestic violence , age at marriage cross tabulation with what type of violence faced, experienced domestic violence in life cross tabulated with does your husband release his anger on daily things, what type of violence cross tabulation with what is the nature of emotional violence, educational qualification cross tabulation with does your husband control your freedom, What type of violence cross tabulated with what is the nature of mental violence, is your husband more angry when he drinks cross tabulated with what are the reasons of domestic violence, educational qualification cross tabulated with how frequent do you face violence, income cross tabulated with how frequent do you face violence, educational qualification cross tabulated with dowry demand at the time of your marriage, dowry demand cross tabulated with what was the demand, is dowry a factor of violence cross tabulated with what is the reason of domestic violence, how frequent do you face violence cross tabulated with what do you think of violence, have you experienced domestic violence in your life violence cross tabulated with what do you think of violence, have you experienced domestic violence cross tabulated with is patriarchy a factor of domestic violence, educational qualification cross tabulated with do you think women opinion is secondary in the family, have you experienced domestic violence cross tabulated with violence affects the women health, educational qualification cross tabulated with illiterate women face more violence then literate, educational qualification cross tabulated with did you ever protest when your husband tortures you, situation of women in Haryana cross tabulated with women of Haryana face more violence than any other state, educational qualification cross tabulated with are you aware of any laws that protect women from violence.

Data Analysis and Interpretation Data Analysis

The total sample is 50 which are individual. The unit of sample is individual. In which i took alcoholic wife 23, non-alcoholic wife 12 and old women are 15 alcoholic and non-alcoholic both.

The total questionnaire is50. The information collected was cross tabulated and SPSS software was used for the data analysis. In data analysis I relate various factors with domestic violence. In this study there are total 77 questions, which were used for collecting the information from the respondents.

Out of 77 questions only 22 questions were cross tabulated. In table 1 and 2 show the number of respondent and their caste. Table 3 caste cross tabulated with educational qualification, age at marriage cross tabulated with domestic violence , age at marriage cross tabulated with what type of violence faced, experienced domestic violence in life cross tabulated with does your husband release his anger on daily things, what type of violence cross tabulation with what is the nature of emotional violence, educational qualification cross tabulation with does your husband controls your freedom, What type of violence cross tabulated with what is the nature of mental violence, does your husband gets more angry when he drinks cross tabulated with what are the reasons of domestic violence, educational qualification cross tabulated with how frequent do you face violence, income cross tabulated with how frequent do you face violence, educational qualification cross tabulated with dowry demand at the time of your marriage, dowry demand cross tabulated with what was the demand, is dowry is a factor of violence cross tabulated with what is the reason of domestic violence, how frequent do you face violence cross tabulated with what do you think of violence, have you experienced domestic violence in your life violence cross tabulated with what do you think of violence, have you experienced domestic violence cross tabulated with is patriarchy is a factor of domestic violence, educational qualification cross tabulated with do you think women opinion is secondary in the family, have you experienced domestic violence cross tabulated with violence affects the women health, educational qualification cross tabulated with illiterate women face more violence then literate, educational qualification cross tabulated with did you ever protest when your husband tortures you, situation of women in Haryana cross tabulated with women of Haryana face more violence then any other state, educational qualification cross tabulated with are you aware of any laws that protect women from to violence.

TABLE 1

No. of Respondents	250

TABLE 2

	General	OBC	SC	ST
Number	65	175	5	5

Enter Caption

From the snowball sampling, it turns out that the population sample mostly belongs to OBC category Yadav Because Bucholi village is Yadav dominated. The other caste is not too much there. So in this study most of the respondent Yadav.

***Caste co-relate with Educational qualification**

Table 3

	Educational Qualification				
Caste	Up to high school	Up to plus two school	Degree and above	No schooling (illiterate)	Total
Gen.	4	1	2	4	65
Obc	13	3	4	17	175
Sc	0	0	0	1	5
St	0	0	1	0	5
Total	17	4	7	22	50

Enter Caption

Caste also affects the educationalal qualification. It was found in the study that the educational qualification differs from caste to caste. As it indicates in the above table, most of the women are illiterate. Educational qualification also affects the violence. Out of 50 respondents, those who are educated too have done their studies only up to high school and did not pursue higher studies further. In interview, mostly women said that they left their study because of the pressure of marriage. The other reason is, their in laws did not allow them to continue their study.

*Age at marriage co-relate with educational qualification

Table 4

Age at marriage	Educational Qualification				Total
	Up to high school	Up to plus two school	Degree and above	No schooling (illiterate)	
Below 18	25	0	0	105	130
18 To 25	60	20	35	5	120
Total	85	20	35	110	**250**

Enter Caption

In table No 4. We can see that the age at marriage also affect the education of women. In this data, it is found that the women who are below 18 they almost are illiterate and on the other hand those who studied only did their high school. After their marriage they left their studies because of not supported by the in laws. The in laws think that female should not work outside their home. There is a big difference between below age 18 and above 25 . In this table, we can see that those women who marry below 18 they are less educated in compared with those women who got married after 18 years.

***Age At marriage Co-Relate With Have You Experienced Domestic violence In your life**

Table 5

		Have you experienced domestic violence in your life	Total
		YES	
Age at marriage	Below 18	130	130
	18 TO 25	120	120
Total		250	250

Enter Caption

In this table, we can see that the percentage of violence is very extreme. Domestic violence is the universal problem. All the respondents said that they have faced/ facing violence. But the reason differs. Some women said that violence happens because of alcohol and the some because of other daily hassles. Daily hassle like unclean cloth, not happy with food. Violence also happens of work related issue. In Bucholi village the ratio of violence is very high. In this study I got 100% result of domestic violence.

***Age at marriage co-relate with what type of violence you have faced?**

Table 6

		What type of violence you have faced		Total
		Mental Violence	All of the above	
Age at marriage	Below 18	0	130	130
	18 to 25	5	115	120
Total		5	245	250

Enter Caption

In this table, we found different types of violence being faced by the women. Violence hurt not only physically but emotionally and psychologically. There are many types of violence in which mental violence, physical violence, verbal abuse and psychological violence are included. Almost respondents said that they have faced all types of violence. Most of the women said that their husband tortures them and abused them. Hit them by anything. 99% of respondent said that they have faced all type of violence.

*Does your Husband release his anger on daily things co relate with have you been slapped by your husband?

Table 7

		Does your husband release his anger on daily things?					
		Not happy with food	Unclean clothes	Work related issue	All of the above	None of the above	Total
Have you been slapped by your husband?	YES	5	5	5	205	20	240
	NO	0	0	0	10	0	10
Total		5	5	5	215	20	250

Enter Caption

In this study, we find that domestic violence against women happens due to the patriarchial nature. The society is male dominated and thus male controls over the woman and he thinks that women is his private property and he can control over the woman. It is also found that, woman are physically beaten by their husbands due to different reasons, like not happy with food, unclean clothes, work related issues. Such reasons are valid for causing physical abuse to their wife. violence happens because a traditional man more expectation from her wife so if she does not have his dinner on the table when he returns home from work even if she also has worked, he believes that she does not care for him.

***Educational Qualification co-relate with does your husband control all your freedom?**
Table 8

		Does your husband control all your freedom?		
		Yes	**No**	**Total**
	Up To High School	80	5	85
	Up To Plus Two School	20	0	20
	Degree And Above	35	0	35
	No Schooling (Illiterate)	110	0	110
Total		245	5	250

Enter Caption

In this table, we can see that most of them had been controlled by their husbands. Their husband doesn't allow them working outside house. Qualification does not matter whether they are literate or illiterate. Women who are literate they are also controlled by their husband. Even some respondents have degree and above qualification they also said that they are not allowed to work outside home, the reason being male dominance. Patriarchy is the main reason of control over the women. They think that women are inferior and male are superior. Women are expected to behave as expected by the society. Most of the respondent said that a female is always under guardianship while single she is under the father and after marriage she comes under the protection of her husband. It's also creating the violence. 99% of women said that they are controlled by their husband.

*What type of violence you have faced co-relate with what is the nature of mental violence?

Table 9

		What Is The Nature Of Mental Violence			
		Feeling worthless	Harm children	Isolation from family	Total
	Mental violence	5	0	0	5
	All of the above	105	110	30	245
Total		110	110	30	250

Enter Caption

In this table we find that, women face domestic violence. All the respondents said that they have faced domestic violence: physical, mental, psychological and verbal violence. In mental violence like feeling worthless they feel that they don't do anything sometimes they think that they are alone. And many respondents said that they feel most of the time to end their life. In mental violence, respondents said that their husband also harm their children and are also isolated from family. Mental violence affects their mind they get tortured by their husband through mental violence. 44% women said that they have feeling of worthlessness in mental violence. 44% said that they harm their children and 12% said that they feel isolated from family.

*Does your husband become more angry when he drinks co-relate with what is the reason of domestic violence

Table 10

		What is the reason of domestic violence?					
		Alcoholism	Dowry	Without any reason	Any other	1 and 2 both	Total
	Yes	125	10	15	25	5	180
	No	0	5	5	60	0	70
Total		125	15	20	85	5	250

Enter Caption

This table shows that women face domestic violence mostly due to the alcohol. In all 80% of the respondents said that their husband become angry when they drink. When they drink, they break things and their temper becomes beyond control. Most of the respondents said that their husband get violent when they are under the influences of alcohol, But when they dont consume alcohol they are very calm. They also help in their domestic work. In this study we can see that there are many reasons of domestic violence. 5% of the women said that they faced violence because of dowry. 2% of the women said that they have faced violence because of both alcohol and dowry. Some respondents said that the reason of domestic violence is extra marital affair, they don't have any child and some said that the demand of the male child is also the reason of domestic violence. In this study respondent said that alcoholism is seen as a stressful experience.

*Educational qualification co-relate with how frequent do you faced violence
Table 11

		How frequent do you face violence?			
		Every Day	Every Week	Every Month	Total
	Up to high school	40	45	0	85
	Up to plus two school	15	0	5	20
	Degree and above	30	5	0	35
	No schooling (illiterate)	90	20	0	110
Total		175	65	5	250

Enter Caption

In this table we see educational qualification with frequency of violence. We cannot say that the women who are illiterate faced more violence. Even the women who are literate they also have faced domestic violence, even they faced violence every day compared to illiterate women. Most of the respondents said that educational qualification doesn't matter because both literate and illiterate faced violence. Only some respondents said that illiterate women faced more violence then literate. Even if she also worked outside the home, the men believe that she does not care for him. This also the reasons of violence. Many women said that it doesn't matter that women is educated or not, they think that if they are not doing work according to her husband, they will be killed by them.

***Income co-relates with how frequent do you faced violence?**

Table 12

		How frequent do you face violence			
		Every Day	Every Week	Every Month	Total
	Below 1 Lakes	80	25	5	110
	1 To 3 (In Lakes)	80	25	0	105
	3 To 5 (In Lakes)	5	15	0	20
	Above 5 Lakes	0	5	0	5
	None Of The Above	10	0	0	10
Total		175	70	5	250

Enter Caption

This table indicates that, violence happen because of income too. In this table, we found that majority of the respondents who faced violence consists income below 1 lakhs, they have faced more violence and after that those which have their income below 3 lakhs they have faced violence every day. Some respondents said that income is also the factor of violence because without money their husband gets frustrated and they get violent on their family member and mostly on their wives.

***Educational qualification co-relate with was there any dowry demand at the time of your marriage?**

Table 13

		Was there any dowry demand at the time of your marriage?		
		Yes	No	Total
	Up to high school	10	75	85
	Up to plus two school	0	20	20
	Degree and above	20	15	35
	No schooling (illiterate)	5	105	110
Total		35	215	250

Enter Caption

In this table we find the demand of dowry system vis-a -vis qualification. Dowry is another reason of domestic violence. Those women who are illiterate are likely that there is no dowry demand at the time of their marriage. The ratio said that mostly, who are graduate and above, the demand for dowry is high. They said that those who are more literate the demand for dowry is high. So there is a fear in the village people that if they educate their girl child, there will be more dowry demand. That is why, they marry their girl almost before 18 by which they can easily avoid dowry. Even most of the people marry their daughter/girl before 12th Class.

***Was there any dowry demand at the time of your marriage co-relate with what was the demand?**

Table 14

	What was the demand				
	Land	Car	Money	Any Other	Total
YES	0	5	25	5	35
NO	215	0	0	0	215
Total	215	5	25	5	250

Enter Caption

In this table we can see that the 14% of respondents said that in their marriage there was dowry demand. And the demand was car, money and other things. Some respondents said that, at the time of their marriage there was demand like television, refrigerator etc. One respondent said that there was demand of gold. Dowry is also a factor of violence. Another respondent said that their in-laws always torture her for dowry. In village people there is a tendency that the people compete on dowry. For instance, if one person gets 1 lakes rupee, then another guy would demand for 1 Lake 50 thousand. So that's why dowry also plays an important role in violence.

***Do you think dowry is a factor of domestic violence co-relate with what is the reason of domestic violence**

TABLE 15

	What Is The Reason Of Domestic Violence?					
	Alcoholism	Dowry	Without any reason	Any Other	1 And 2 Both	Total
YES	125	15	20	85	5	250
No	0	0	0	0	0	0
Total	125	15	20	85	5	250

Enter Caption

In this table we can see that 100% respondent views on dowry being the factor for domestic violence. Dowry discriminates women. They facedviolence due to the dowry system. Dowry is a social evil for our society, it even leads to kill women. In this study it is found that, many women are made out from the house through their in-laws and their husband. In the above table, we see that 50% of the women faced violence because of alcoholism. Due to the alcoholism women are physically harmed. Respondents said that whenever their husband comes home they fight with them. Many respondents said that because of violence they are forced to leave their own parents house for some months and years. They do nothing without their husband's permission and are completely under control. Some respondents said that their husband gets violent without any reason, they just want to control their wives. Many respondents said that there is many other reasons like affair with another women, impotent, son preference which aggravates violence

*How frequent do you face violence co-relate with what do you think of violence
Table 16

		What do you think of violence?		
		Bad	Not acceptable	Total
	Every Day	170	5	175
	Every Week	70	0	70
	Every Month	5	0	5
Total		245	5	250

Enter Caption

In this table we find that, above 80% women faced violence every day. Most of the women said that alcohol is the biggest problem. And 15 % said that they faced every week. All the respondents said that violence is not fair . Women want to commit suicide by being frustrated facing violence. Respondents said that their husband always want to control them. Even they don't like their wives talking to another person but they do whatever they want to do. In village even they don't allow to participate in functions and *Ladies Sangeet*. Violence is bad for not only for women but for society as a whole. Because violence affects family members to a large extent. Children's education also gets affected. Some respondents said that violence is shocking and horrible.

***Have you experienced domestic violence in your life co-relate with do you think patriarchy is a factor of violence?**

Table 17

	Do you think patriarchy is a factor of violence? Yes	Total
Yes	250	250
No	0	0
Total	250	250

Enter Caption

In this table we see that, all the respondents have faced violence in their life. They all have experienced violence whether it is physical, mental, verbal etc. Among all, 100 % respondents said that patriarchy is a factor of violence. Patriarchy plays an important role in domestic violence. Indian society is male dominant society where male is the head of the house. Women are controlled by their husbands. They avail no freedom. Many respondents said that all the restrictions are made for the women. Male are free for doing whatever they want. In rural areas this male control is never throughout. Some respondents said that patriarchy means that they have no control over her own self. They said that all decisions regarding their body is made by their husband.

*Educational qualification co-relate with do you think women's decision is secondary in the family

Table 18

		Do you think women's opinion and decision is secondry in the family?		Total
		Yes	No	
	Up to high School	80	5	85
	Up to plus two school	20	0	20
	Degree and above	30	5	35
	No schooling (illiterate)	110	0	110
Total		48	2	250

Enter Caption

In this table we can see that, women's decision is secondary in the family. Most of the respondents said that they have no access to decision making ,as most of the time they don't know the decisions taken by their husbands. Respondents said that even if they want to take part in the decision of their husband, they are not allowed to take. We see that the educational qualification of the women doesn't matter. She is not given decision making power. In village Male feel that they are superior than female that's why they take all the decisions. Even in the case of working women, the decision making head is her husband.

*Have you experienced domestic violence in your life co-relate with do you think domestic violence affects the women's health?

Table 19

		Do you think domestic violence affects the women's health	Total
		Yes	
	Yes	250	250
Total		250	250

Enter Caption

In this study we can see that all the respondents have experienced domestic violence. In Bucholi village most of the women said that the violence happens because of alcohol, without alcohol their husband doesn't get violent. Violence affects the entire family bond, children educational etc. This also affects women's health. Many of the respondents said that they have faced violence since 10 to 20 years so it has tremendous effect on health and they get weak. When they are faced with such tortures by their husband they attempt to take acid, poison and some drink like Phenyl too. Most of the old women said that they stopped talking to each other even for a span of 10 to 20 years.

***Educationalqualification co-relates with do you think literate women face more violence than/with literate?**

Table 20

	Do you think illiterate women face more violence than literate			
	Yes	No	Can't Say	Total
Up to high school	4	5	8	17
Up to plus two school	0	1	3	4
Degree and above	2	4	1	7
No schooling (illiterate)	3	12	7	22
Total	9	22	19	50

Enter Caption

The above table indicates, violence happens with both women who are literate and who are illiterate. Women with degree and above also said that they faced violence every day. It has nothing to do with educational qualification. This village is patriarchial in nature where the head of the family is male. They think that women are obliged for do the household work and taking care of the children.

*Educational qualification co-relate with did you ever protest when your husband tortures you

Table 21

		Did you ever protest when your husband tortures you		Total
		Yes	No	
	Up to high school	70	15	85
	Up to plus two school	20	0	20
	Degree and above	25	10	35
	No Schooling (Illiterate)	70	40	110
Total		185	65	250

Enter Caption

In this study we found that educated and uneducated women protest when their husband tortures them. in this study we found that majority of the women protest against their husband's violence. Some respondents express that they do not protest because they think that it's the right of the man. And some educated woman express that they do not protest against their husband due to the family pressure because if they protest against husband it's shameful for her parents. Some respondents said that if they protest their husband gets more violent. So for such reason some woman cannot protest against their husband. 74% respondent said that they have protested against their husband.

26% respondent say no because they said if they protest against their husband her family members said that "Ladki k sath uske kutumb ki izzat judi hue hai."

***What is the situation of women in Haryana co-relate with do you think women of Haryana face more violence than any other state**

Table 22

		Do you think women of haryana face more violence then any other state				
		Yes	No	Can't Say	May Be	Total
	Bad	85	0	25	0	110
	Average	15	0	25	0	40
	Both bad and good	5	5	80	10	100
Total		105	5	130	10	250

Enter Caption

Indicates the situation of woman in Haryana state. As we know Haryana is one of the state in which the situation of woman is worse. We also know that condition of woman is very bad because of the patriarchial dominance in the state. In this study it is found that majority of the respondents express that situation of woman in Haryana is very bad .Woman are exploited by man, woman have no liberty and freedom in this society.

*What is the situation of women in Haryana co-relate with do you think women of Haryana face more violence than any other state

Table 22

		Do you think women of haryana face more violence then any other state				
		Yes	No	Can't Say	May Be	Total
	Bad	85	0	25	0	110
	Average	15	0	25	0	40
	Both bad and good	5	5	80	10	100
Total		105	5	130	10	250

Enter Caption

In this table we can see if women are aware of the laws that might protect women from violence. In this study, we found that majority of the woman said they are not aware of any law that protect woman from violence. Many respondents said that they are educated and they know the law but they do not go for it because they fear of insult or social stigma.

5

Discussion and Conclusion

Domestic violence is the most serious violation of a woman's fundamental rights that she faces in her own home at the hands of family members. Data and in-depth work done by several people in the women"s movement have systematically exposed to many problems associated with domestic violence. Indeed, the home has been identified as a site of violence against women and girls in recent studies by the Family Health Survey and the National Crimes Record Bureau. A young married woman is burnt alive, beaten to death, or forced to commit suicide almost every six hours somewhere in India.

Violence is shocking, horrible and life threatening. Violence is an expression of aggression. Violence can impact various forms of human life whether men, women or children (Krantz Gunilla, 2005)

Abuse can take many forms and violence is one of them. Violence is the use of physical force or power against a person. Violence is the form of the abusive behavior. For example abusive behavior happen in many ways like in verbal abuse, a person put downs another person. Like- how can you be so stupid, you look so ugly etc,.It uses threats and manipulation etc. Violence is the sub-category of abuse. Violence is a form of physical abuse. It generally refer to the act of harming another person (Eisikovits, 2000)

Mental abuse is a form of violence that affects the mind, often leaving the abused feeling worthless and lacking empowerment.. Threat, Fear, threat to harm children, Isolation from family and friends, Loss of social contact, Persistent criticism, denial of privacy, verbal abuse, deprivation of sleep, money, clothes, going out, use of telephone, terror and intimidation

Physical violence is called as aggressive acts such as throwing things, kicking, slapping, hitting, Pushing, shoving, grabbing, Choking, strangling, suffocating, using a weapon, bruising, breaking bones, cuts, scratches, Bitting, burnt, scalded, Knocking unconscious, Miscarriage due to violence,throwing Chemical on face, and death. In the physical violence women are injured seriously and in some cases are dead. According a studied from various part of the world shows that between 10 per cent and 60 per cent of the women had been hit and physically assaulted by their male partner

Verbal abuse occurs when "one person uses any words or body language to inappropriately criticize another person," observed Patricelli. (Abrahams, 2007) Verbal abuse is characterized as a mental abuse because the abuser will taunt the abused, making her feel unloved and unworthy of respect. Verbal abusing also painful and damaging and it's also affecting the women life. In verbal abuse you feel afraid and powerless. Verbal abuse includes name calling, putting you down, rejecting your opinions, insulting, blaming and mocking

Emotional abuse is a type of abuse in which ones play with someone's emotions. There is many ways in which your partner control and manipulate your emotions. In emotional violence include the yelling or swearing, name calling, insult, ignoring. This type of violence is difficult to define like; husband forces to his wife to have sex

Damage to personal property, theft of property, threats and violence to pets, animals, denied access to work.Domestic violence happens in personal relationship domestic violence is abusive behavior in which a partner controls another partner. It may happen between current partner, girlfriend and boyfriend, men and women of any religion and any race affected by domestic violence. But most of its victims are women. Violence is the big problem facing by our society today. Alcohol playing a important role in these violence. Hence we can say that violent behaviour is like as drinking behaviour, violence happens both physical and mental. Violence against women is being recognized as an important public health concern. Emotional sexual and physical violence by an intimate male partner is one of the most common forms it takes In India, where family structure is patriarchal, patrilocal and patrilineal, women are particularly vulnerable to violence.

Patriarchy plays an important role in domestic violence. Due to patriarchy violence happens. Patriarchy is a Greek word. its mean the role of the father. Where the male dominated society. According to Radical feminist, "It is analysis of gender inequality in which men as a group dominate women as a group and are the main beneficiaries of the subordination of women. This system of domination is called patriarchy" (Walby Sylvia, 198). According to Sylvia, patriarchy provides a system of control and law and order. She also interlinked patriarchy and capitalist. Both capitalist and patriarchy, argues that both system are present and important in the structuring of contemporary gender relations. Capitalist and patriarchy are two system that are so closed, patriarchy provides a system of control and law and order, while capitalism provides a system of economy, the pursuit of profit

The violence against women also increases because of alcohol. Women go through violence because her husband is habitual of consumption of alcohol. This excessive drinking leads to partner violence. There is a big relation between alcohol and violence. 1991 National Criminal Victimization Survey perceived more than one fourth of violent criminal to be under the influences of alcohol (Robert and Kathleen, 1998). Many studies relate to violence and alcohol consumption. A study in Brazil found that alcohol consumption increases the violent behavior and the anger of a person also increases. A population based study in Brazil found that aggressor was under the influence of alcohol at the time of the event in over half of the identified cases of domestic violence. Violence becomes more power with increased alcohol consumption. Alcohol is the risk for the violent behavior because it has direct effects on physical, alcohol reducing self-control, reducing judgments, reducing the ability to recognize signs of danger. Alcohol affects the family members, children and other relatives influenced by alcoholism. Many cases of domestic violence happen due to jealousy if the spouses are either suspected or being unfaithful.

According to NAFVS (National Alcohol and Family Violence Survey 1992) the empirical evidence shows that the linkage between drinking and wife beating are not a problem of poor ethnic minorities. Domestic violence due to alcohol consumptions are recognized as major public health problems. Domestic violence and alcohol both are biological, psychological and sociological factors. Alcohol consumption is the third leading risk factor for illness and disabilities worldwide (WHO)

This study found that the entire respondents are victim of violence. There are many reasons for domestic violence: alcohol, dowry, daily hassle and much other reason. All the respondent said that they are always controlled by the men and women have no choice to doing anything, Prem chowdhry (2007) also said that a female is always under guardianship whether she is single or married. 100 per cent respondent said that patriarchy is a factor of domestic violence. 100 per cent respondent said that a traditional man have more expectation from her wife, walker (2017) also said that a traditional man have more expectation from her wife this is also the reason of violence. In this study most of the respondent said that through patriarchy women are also under the control. Walby Sylvia (1986) said that patriarchy provide a system of control and law and order.

violence we can say that, violence is universal, it is a sensitive issue. Domestic violence is a worldwide problem. In this study we found that domestic violence happens because of many reasons like, alcoholism, dowry, extra marital affair, expectation of boy child, no child etc. in this study all the respondent said that they faced domestic violence. Some respondent said that they faced violence because of alcohol. Some said that they faced it because of dowry. Most of the women said that patriarchy is a main factor of the violence. The village in this study is patriarchal in nature. The entire respondent said that all the decisions are taken by male members of the family. Women are not given chance in decision making because they are not allowed to take decisions . Male members of the family think that women are not active in decision making. They think that women are only meant for doing all the domestic works. They don't allow them to go out from the house and get a job, female are controlled by male. They think that women are like their property only. Most of the women said that they faced all type of violence like, physical,mental, psychological and verbal violence. Respondents said that violence also happens because male members are unhappy with food items cooked by the females in the household, they get annoyed for their clothes not cleaned by their wife .husband of the female thinks that they are always correct and their wives are wrong. Their husband controls their freedom, Even they do not like that their wives are talking with another person. Some respondent said that the perpetrators of violence are also their sons. Some women are tortured by their sons.

In this study we see that even educated women are also the victims of the domestic violence. All the literate or illiterate women face violence. Violence also influences their health. Due to domestic violence some women feel suicidal tendency due to the sufferings of domestic violence. Some respondents said that they attempted suicide but were rescued by someone in the family. Domestic violence is a big problem. Many of the women in different places died of violence. Even the literate women do not take any action towards their husband because they are pressurized by their own family. Her own parents said that if she complaint about her husband and returns back to her parents home then it will bring bad name to her parents in the society. In this study the majority of violence is due to alcohol. Alcohol is one of the major problem and it's creating domestic violence. Many older women said that they did not conversate with their husband since 10 to 12 years because of facing violence and torture by their husbands.Most of the respondenst said that unemployment also creates violence because due to unemployment, their husband gets frustrated and their anger is released on their wives. Some women are tortured because they have no children and their family blames only to the female. Their family said that women is only responsible for the infertility . In this study most of the victims are scared that if they go against their husband their husband will be more violent. In this study it is found that patriarchy is the factor of violence and women are tortured by their partners. Their husband think that they are supreme and women are inferior.

Suggestions

1. Alcohol should be banned. Need to close bars, belt shops and other places where alcohol is available than there should be control over on alcoholic based domestic violence.
2. There should be control over on content of media which promote violence and sexual based violence due to pornography and other sites.
3. There should be efficient and accountable law enforcement at all levels through administration, government, police and judiciary. Need of women police who can deal effectively against the cruelty of domestic violence. every police station should have trained women police for the action of domestic violence
4. There should be moral and religious teachings for all level age people by that they may get awareness on

domestic violence

5. Education and employment play vital role to eradicate domestic violence so let there should be education to all at free of cost
6. Financial independence is the major tool to eradicate domestic violence. She won't be dependent on her partner for finance and other economical things. Women should be economically empowered through education and job.
7. There should be code of conduct at home, work place and schools with opposite sex regarding interaction and any related work
8. There should be special gender sensitization education to all the people through playing videos, audios and other possible ways at all the areas such as public gathering places, bus stands, railway stations, airports and schools.

6

REFERENCES

Abrahams Hilary. (2007) Supporting Women after Domestic Violence, London: Jessica Kingsley.

Begleiter Henri et-al. (2002) Alcohol and violence, New York, London: Kluwer Academic publisher.

Bhasin, Kamla. (2000) Understanding Gender,New Delhi: Women Unlimited. Davis Cathy. (2003) Housing Association-Rehousing Women Leaving Domestic Violence, Great Britain: The Policy Press.

Davis, N.J. (1998)Battered women: Implications for social control. Contemporary Crises 12, 345–372

Dugan Meg et al. (2000) It's My Life Now, New York: Routledge Publisher.

EisikovitsZvi et al. (2000) A Violent Embrace, London: Sage publication.

Hackett, T. Michelle. (2011) Domestic Violence Against Women: Statistical Analysis.

Jackson.K.Joan. (1958) Alcoholism and Family, America: Sage publication.

Krantz, Gunilla. (2005) Violence Against Women, London: BMJ Publication.

Lerner, Gerda. (1986) The Creation Of Patriarchy, Oxford University Press, New York.

Mullender Andrew. (1996) Rethinking Domestic Violence, London &New York: Taylor and Francis group.
Parker Robert et al. (1998) Alcohol Drugs and Violence,California: Annual Reviews.

Sharma, K. Behind closed doors: domestic violence in India. Fem Rev 83, 169–171 (2006)

Walby Sylvia. (1990) Theorizing Patriarchy, UK: Basil Blackwell.

Walker, Lenore. (2017) The Bettered Woman Syndrome, New York: Springer.

WHO. (2005) Women's Health and Domestic Violence Against Women, Switzerland: WHO library.

7

Appendix

Annexure 1

consists the questionnaire used for data collection.

Section I. Basic information of the respondent

1 .Date:

2. Time:

3. Name:

4. Age:

5. Caste:

6. Ageat marriage

7. Marriage:

(i) Love marriage ( ) (ii) Arrange Marriage ( )

(A) Elope ( )

(B) Proper wedding ( )

8. Educational: (i) up to high school ( ) (ii) Up to plus two ( ) (iii) Degree and above ( ) (iv) No schooling (illiterate) ( )

9. Employment:

(i) Employed ( ) (ii) Unemployed ( ) (iii) Self- Employed (pvt.) ( )

10. Family type

(i) Joint family ( ) (ii) Nuclear family ( )

11. No. of children:

12. Income:

13. Husband name:

14. Husband Occupation:

15. Mobile-No:

16. Who is the bread winner in your family?

(i) Husband ( ) (ii) Son ( ) (iii) Father ( ) (iv) Mother ( ) (v) You ( ) 41 SectionII. Information on the perception of violence?

17. Have you experienced domestic violence in your life?

(i) Yes ( ) (ii) No ( ) If yes then continue.......................................

18. What type of violence you have faced?

(i) Physical violence ( ) (ii) Mental violence ( ) (iii) Psychological violence ( ) (iv) Verbal abuse ( )

19. Does your partner threaten to harm you?

(i) Yes ( ) (ii) No ( )

20. Have you been hit by your husband?

(i) Yes ( ) (ii) No ( )

21. What is the nature of physical violence?

(i) Belts ( ) (ii) Burnt ( ) (iii) Cuts ( ) (iv) Choking ( ) (v) All the above ( )

22. Have you been kicked by your husband?

(i) Yes ( ) (ii) No ( )

23. Have you been slapped by your husband?

(i) Yes ( ) (ii) No ( )

24. Does your husband strike you with his hands or feet?

(i) Yes ( ) (ii) No ( )

25. Does your husband ever threaten you with an object?

(i) Yes ( ) (ii) No ( )

26. Has your husband ever scolded/insulted you in front of the people?

(i) Yes ( ) (ii) No ( )

27. Does your husband ever break things when he is angry?

(i) Yes ( ) (ii) No ( )

28. Does your husband release his anger on daily things like:

(i) Not happy with food ( ) (ii) Unclear Clothes ( ) (iii) work related issue ( ) (iv)All of the above ( ) (v) none of the above ( )

29. Does your husband feel he is always right?

(i) Yes ( ) (ii) No ( ) (iii) Can't say ( ) (iv) Maybe ( )

30. What is the nature of emotional violence?

(i) Insult ( ) (ii) Ignoring ( ) (iii) Name calling ( ) (iv) Anyother ( ) (v) All of the above ( )

31. Have you been ignored by your husband?

(i) Yes ( ) (ii) No ( )

32. Does your husband control all your freedom?

(i) Yes ( ) (ii) No ( ) (iii) Can't say ( ) (iv) Maybe ( )

33. Does your husband manipulate your emotions?

(i) Yes ( ) (ii) No ( ) (iii) Can't say ( ) (iv) Maybe ( )

34. What is the nature of mental violence?

(i) Feeling worthless ( ) (ii) Harm children ( ) (iii) Isolation from family ( ) (iv) Loss of social control ( )

35. Have you ever felt isolated and alone?

(i) Yes ( ) (ii) No ( ) (iii) Can't say ( ) (iv) Maybe ( )

36. Has your husband ever violent towards your children?

(i) Yes ( ) (ii) No ( ) (iii) Can't say ( ) (iv) Maybe ( )

37. Does your husband become angrier when he drinks?

(i) Yes ( ) (ii) No ( ) (iii) Can't say ( ) (iv) Maybe ( )

38. Do you think he is more violent when he is drunk?

(i) Yes ( ) (ii) No ( ) (iii) Can'tsay ( ) (iv) Maybe ( )

39. How frequent do you face violence?

(i) Every day ( ) (ii) Every week ( ) (iii) Every month ( ) (iv) Any other ( )

40. Who is the Perpetrators' of violence in the family?

(i) Husband only ( ) (ii) Mother –in-law ( ) (iii) Father-in-law ( ) (iv) Sister-in-law ( )

(v) Brother-in-law ( ) (vi) All the above ( )

41. What are the reasons/reasons of domestic violence?

(i) Alcoholism ( ) (ii) dowry ( ) (iii) Without any reason ( ) (iv) Any other ( )

42. Was there any dowry demand at the time of your marriage?

(i) Yes ( ) (ii) No ( ) If yes...

43. What was the demand?

(i) Car ( ) (ii) money ( ) (iii) Land ( ) (iv) anyother ( )

44. Do you think dowry is a factor of domestic violence?

(i) Yes ( ) (ii) No ( ) (iii) can't say ( ) (iv) maybe ( )

45. What do you think of violence?

(i) Good ( ) (ii) Bad ( ) (iii) Acceptable ( ) (iv) Not acceptable ( )

46. Do you think violence affects the whole family?

(i) Yes ( ) (ii) No ( ) (iii) Can'tsay ( ) (iv) Maybe ( )

47. Do you think patriarchy is a factor of violence?

(i) Yes ( ) (ii) No ( ) (iii) can't say ( ) (iv) maybe ( )

48. Do you think women are exploited at home?

(i) Yes ( ) (ii) No ( ) (iii) can't say ( ) (iv) maybe ( )

49. Do you think women enjoy less autonomy then men in the family?

(i) Yes ( ) (ii) No ( ) (iii) can't say ( ) (iv) may be ( )

50. Do you think women's opinion and decision is secondary in the family?

(i) Yes ( ) (ii) No ( ) (iii) can't say ( ) (iv) may be ( )

51. Do you think wife beating is good or bad?

(i) Yes ( ) (ii) No ( ) (iii) can't say ( ) (iv) may be ( )

52. Do you agree wife beating is right for men?

(i) Agree ( ) (ii) Don't agree ( ) (iii) Can't say ( )

53. Do you think girls have more restrictions then boys in the family?

(i) Yes ( ) (ii) No ( ) (iii) can't say ( ) (iv) may be ( )

54. Do you think alcohol aggravates violence against women?

(i) Yes ( ) (ii) No ( ) (iii) can't say ( ) (iv) may be ( )

55. Do you think domestic violence affect the women's health?

(i) Yes ( ) (ii) No ( ) (iii) can't say ( ) (iv) maybe ( )

56. Do you think domestic violence effect the children Educational?

(i) Yes ( ) (ii) No ( ) (iii) can't say ( ) (iv) maybe ( )

57. Do you think violence happens because of male domination?

(i)Yes ( ) (ii) No ( )

58. Who decides in your family?

(i) Father ( ) (ii) Mother ( ) (iii) Husband ( ) (iv) Son ( ) (v) In-laws ( )

59. Do you think illiterate women face more violence than literate?

(i) Yes ( ) (ii) No ( ) (iii) can't say ( ) (iv) maybe ( )

60. Do you think socialization is a factor of domestic violence?

(i) Yes ( ) (ii) No ( ) (iii) can't say ( ) (iv) maybe ( )

61. Do you think alcohol leads to violence in the family?

(i) Yes ( ) (ii) No ( ) (iii) can't say ( ) (iv) maybe ( )

62. Do you think female is controlled by men?

(i) Yes ( ) (ii) No ( ) (iii) can't say ( ) (iv) maybe ( ) .

63. Is patriarchal more prone to domestic violence?

(i) Yes (ii) No ( ) (iii) can't say (iv) may be

64. Do you think man take all the decision of women's body?

(i) Yes ( ) (ii) No(iii) can'tsay (iv) may be

65. Do you think man impose their power because of masculinity?

(i) Yes ( ) (ii) No ( ) (iii) can't say (iv) May be ( )

66. Do you think traditional man have more expectation from his wife?

(i) Yes ( ) (ii) No ( ) (iii) can'tsay ( ) (iv) maybe ( )

67. Do you think more expectation also creates violence?

(i) Yes ( ) (ii) No ( ) (iii) Can't say ( ) (iv) may be ( )

68. Did you ever protest when your husband tortures you?

(i) Yes ( ) (ii) No ( ) (iii) Can't say ( ) (iv) May be ( )

69. Did you get any help from your any of the following?

(i) In-laws ( ) (ii) Social support ( ) (iii) Neighbors ( ) (iv) your own parents/family

70. Is your in-laws supportive enough there is family issue?

(i) Yes ( ) (ii) No () (iii) Can't say ( ) (iv) Maybe ( )

71. Do you think men also gets tortured by women?

(i) Yes ( ) (ii) No ( ) (iii) Can't say ( ) (iv) May be

72. What is the situation of women in Haryana?

(i) Good ( ) (ii) Bad ( ) (iii) Average ( ) (iv) Both bad and good ( )

73. Do you think women of Haryana faced more violence than any other state?

(i) Yes ( ) (ii) No ( ) (iii) Can't say ( ) (iv) May be ( )

74. Do you think women are treated as housewife in Haryana?

(i) Yes ( ) (ii) No ( ) (iii) Can't say ( ) (iv) Maybe ( )

75. Are you aware of any laws that protect women from to violence?

(i) Yes ( ) (ii) No ( )

76. Are you aware of any provisions that would help you to take support?

(i) Yes ( ) (ii) No ( )

77. Are you aware of this provision "The protection of women from domestic violence Act 2005"?

(i) Yes ( ) (ii) No (

Printed by Libri Plureos GmbH in Hamburg, Germany